To Carve a Path Through Thickets

To Carve a Path Through Thickets

Poems by

Merryn Rutledge

Cover design by Shay Culligan
Cover image by Julia Ly on Unsplash

ISBN: 979-8-90146-726-8
Library of Congress Control Number: 2026935827

Kelsay Books
502 South 1040 East, A-119
American Fork, Utah 84003
Kelsaybooks.com

Acknowledgments

Grateful acknowledgment to the editors of publications where poems have appeared, sometimes in earlier versions or with different titles.

Blood & Bourbon: "Retroflection"

The Ilanot Review: "Lost in Translation," "To Fly"

Last Stanza Poetry Journal: "*Gaman*—Meaning *to Preserve,*" "The Man Interviewed on the Radio After the Christmas Blizzard in Buffalo"

The Marbled Sigh: "Here Remembering Araju, Killed at 17"

Massachusetts Bards Poetry Anthologies (2024 and 2025): "Life Lessons," "Perspective"

MIDLVLMAG: "Economy"

The MockingOwl Roost: "Simpatico"

Moss Piglet: "Grace on Saturday Morning"

Naugatuck River Review: "Rust" (finalist, best narrative poem contest, 2024)

Northern New England Review: "Reckoning"

Pensive Journal: "Hildegard in Her Workshop"

Persimmon Tree: "What's in a Name"

Poemeleon: "Grace on Saturday Morning," "Understudy"

Portrait of New England: "Setting Out"

Pure Slush, Lifespan Anthology Series: "Losing It"

Red Wolf Editions, Recovering Greenness: An Anthology of Poems: "All the Green"

The Soliloquist: "Quiet," "Return Flight"

Songs of Eretz Poetry Review: "At New View Stone, Inc."

Synkroniciti Magazine: "Earth, Breath, Water, Fire," "Figure and Ground," "Forgiveness," "In Her Choir," "Questions" (nominated for Best of the Net, 2023), "Reckoning," "Stained Glass in Köln," "Trying to Imagine, March 2022"

t'Art: "Lunch at the Food Kitchen"

WayWards Literary Journal: "Ghosted"

Young Ravens Literary Review: "Designs for Life," "Joan of Arc's Testament"

Thanks also to True Grit Art Gallery, Middleboro, MA, for including "Figure and Ground" in an exhibition in which artists created pieces based on selected poems.

Gratitude to my teachers: Ellen Bass, Bruce Beasely, Mark S. Burroughs, Peter Campion, and Dorianne Laux.

Editing by Brett Warren.

Permissions:

Contents

I.
In Memory Blooming

Setting Out

For my father, Lloyd Lafayette (1918–2012),
who as a boy was called "Fate"

He left home with a cast iron skillet,
matches, a little flour, lard, and Voyd Videll Curtis Caldwell,
who would follow him anywhere.
Joining them were three schoolmates ripe for adventure.
Fate had been reading Thoreau, whose experiment
he aimed to adapt to wilder conditions in the Ozarks.
Used to woods and solitary work,
Fate imagined he had already tasted a little
of *the marrow of life* the Walden man was after.
Miss Troy, the teacher who brought him the Concord sages,
also confirmed that you had to reflect
on your experiences in order to effect a deepening.
Then there was no telling what would unfold.

The boys hiked as the long, spring day unspooled.
By the time they decided they were far enough
from the one-street hamlet of their civilization,
they were famished.
Gnarly blackberry patch nearby and the bears had left some.
The boys built a fire and baked a gooey cobbler,
juice turning to candy from a little scorching.

As dusk swooped in, Fate invited the others to think
about what becoming a leader entailed. Voyd guffawed,
chiding his friend for staying so serious. Fate grinned
and eased up in favor of owl entertainment.
Lying down beside the others,
it came to him that this was what he wanted to do—

guide boys and girls on adventures,
like how to feed a fire-lit soul and carve a path
through thickets that lay between them and being grown.
In the meantime, he determined to stay awake
with the creatures stirring around him,
watching for ways to venture into the dark.

Gaman—Meaning *to Persevere*

After the documentary "Amache" (Denver Botanical Garden, 2024), about Japanese Americans imprisoned at the Amache camp in Colorado, 1942–1945, the remnants of which were recently discovered

Pink, the anthropologist mutters when she sees
the furled blossom peeking over a cinder block wall
that crumbles into prairie.
Pink. As though christening the first flower
seen on scraggy bushes planted eighty years before.

An old woman stoops beside her, remembering
when she set the fragile roots
in barren sand enriched with chicken droppings,
composted carrot tops, potato peels,
and melon vines from her husband's garden.
A garden he had grown to enliven
palate-numbing camp food
and relieve eyes longing for green.

Roses had risen to paint in pink dignity
the whole square mile of desert jail.
Blossoms proclaimed a reclamation,
coloring the government's name—Relocation Center—
as though the prisoners and their neighbors
had merely been resettled into new homes.
As though no racism borne for generations
had befallen them.

The anthropologist kneels beside the flower
where long ago the rose gardener had knelt,
shading the tender plant from sun
that seared face and hands.
She had mounded earth to make a well for water.

Looking back on that time,
the old gardener recalls what she thought back then,
Shikata ga nai—It cannot be helped; it is what it is.

Even now the rose is as it is
and in memory blooming.
Roses, all who labored here.

Trying to Imagine, March 2022

A traveler spotting a girl's small sandal
beside a dusty Arkansas road   would have wondered
at the tiny toe—and heel-print smudges on loose innersoles
Where was the child

The surprising jolt when my parents said
No   they would not turn back   *Stop crying*   *It's only a shoe*
The bolt snapped when Father's hand had turned the house key
We left for good   *I lived*   I could tell the wondering traveler now

Now   together we wonder
We fear for the millions   women   children   men
who bleed from Ukraine   now exploding

Cars crawl   women trudge along highways
Children whine and wail
Mothers dangle the youngest from their hips
hold in mind loved ones left behind
the friendly houses   rows of books
framed photos taken before or after
the Great War   the famine   the Second World War

The procession passes roller suitcases   broken   open-mouthed
or too heavy to lug the long way to the border
a limp doll   face-down in a puddle
a blank-faced Spider-Man   one arm raised
an overturned stroller with a busted wheel
Where is the child

In school I knew a girl who fled Hungary in 1956
She was six

They crouched through underbrush   in the dark
cold pricking her bare legs

Keep still   her father mouthed   *Don't even whisper*
until we get across
She thought she heard Kitty   meowing
in the kitchen   back home   in a box
with sides too high for him to jump

Soon Papa would grab her hand and run   run so fast
he would   jerk her   into the air   drag her
Her arm would always ache

Grace on Saturday Morning

I will remember their care as I prepare
a feast from the bounty now carefully handled by a woman
who hums as she packs my groceries. My serious cashier
with shining eyes and silver hair. A strong-boned
face a sculptor—or a lover—would like to gaze on.
The whistling man in produce who showed me the bottled
horseradish I would not have found on my own.
Behind the deli counter, the server sang out,
Good morning before artfully arranging chicken chunks
that a cook in the hidden kitchen grilled just so.
I tell Adonis I have two more jugs of water
like the one I've heaved, with difficulty, onto the counter.
Trusting me, he solemnly nods and blesses the water
three times with his scanner.

Economy

A bright orange I bought this morning spills
blossom-scented juice and a cache of questions.
Who rose at dawn in rising heat and rode
a crowded bus to pick from rows of trees?
Who ferried loads to the packing plant
where *señores* and *señoras* stood for hours
culling fruit, heaving crates?
What truckers fought to stay awake
to bring the harvest east to us, the winter-weary?
This morning, in the store, the man building
perfect pyramids of fruit was singing.
He looked my way and switched to English.
Miss, what can I help you find? He smiled.
Thank you, I might have said.

Neither a Borrower nor a Lender Be

Just as the cork fattens, my old corkscrew handle
cracks. Having cooked all day, I'm already tired,
my first time as a solo host.

Entertaining was so easy when there were two of us.
But he is gone. Breathless, I run to my neighbor Jeanne,
who disappears and hurries back with just what I need.

My mother, sifting flour, would find herself short
on sugar, a margarine stick, or an egg.
She'd send me to ask next door or up the street.

Later I'd carry a mounded plate to our donor—
warm cookies, spicy, communally conceived.
Next time, we'd be the ones to fill their pantry.

Tonight the wine sighs as my guests tumble in
bearing gifts—more wine, and flowers I'll share
with Jeanne. Complete the circle, keep the tribe alive.

Apple Picking

Past strip malls and stoplights,
up the ribbon of road into Appalachian foothills
where the orchards were,
the station wagon crammed with us five kids
and stacks of bushel baskets
that held the cidery scent of last year's apples.
My eyes filled with fallow fields,
tall pines, flaming maples,
I dozed, tomorrow's homework as hazy
as the mountains ahead.

Mom and Dad stopped to greet the orchard owner,
a ritual they learned growing up on farms.
Fine weather this year! What a day.
They wended their way to asking about the crop,
then smiled at the farmer's assurances.

We bumped up dirt tracks
between rows of trees heavy with blushing fruit,
and tumbled out into an Eden
where even a pup like me could reach and twist apples free.
I moved slowly among the yellow jackets
sucking sugar while I grazed
among dew-glistening, new-fallen apples.
I gathered a lapful in the front of my shirt.

My parents put away arguing on these trips.
They seemed to have settled
that this was the day and the harvest, enough.
I wonder now if perhaps, inside each of them,
they kept the store of rare days
when their own work-driven parents
created a holiday.

Lunch at the Food Kitchen

Already the pizza is gone,
yet strings of hungry people keep fraying
into the room. I tell the next person we have bologna
sandwiches, frozen because the refrigerator was turned
too low. *Can't eat pork.* She frowns.

A paper towel, please, a man asks,
swabbing his sweat-wet face with napkins
that shred like skin coming loose.

I scan the lines searching for the thin young man
who first showed up last week,
whispering, *Jamon? Jamon?* I didn't understand.
How did he make his way this far north,
and from where? Where can he be?

Many folks ask for bottled water as we all unravel
in the heat. I turn to Sandy, the cook.
Has the shelter suggested that donors pack water
in the lunch bags? *We've had congregations stop giving
when we ask.* Her pursed lips say, *Can you believe?*

Today's load of lunches came with pamphlets tucked in
with a no-mayo sandwich and chips.
Come to Jesus. Let Him Heal. Be Saved!
Charity makes its claim.

Questions

Joseph Washington, born in North Carolina 1857, a slave
Died Massachusetts 1881, FREE. To the faithful, reward is certain
—Headstone, town cemetery, Hanover, Massachusetts

How came you to this little town
of farmers, merchants, builders of boats?
Did you travel alone, with family or friends?
Did Robert, the Union veteran who lies nearby,
carry you north at war's end?
For love, or mercy's sake? Or as the victor's prize, to serve him?

You died so young. I would like to know how.
Perhaps you took sick or had an accident.
Was early death an inheritance—
insides knotted with your sold-South daddy's grief
or bones thinned by White babies
who stole your mother's milk?

Town historians refashioned you as a footnote—
Lived in the family of Robert, Saba and Effie Church—
neighbors here beside you for eternity.
Did they love you for yourself?
Did they pen the epitaph?

Was *FREE* your loud, proud claim
or a presumptive boast by those who carved this stone?
And the pious summing of your life—
To the faithful, reward is certain—
could you be faithful to yourself?

Did you push a lathe or plow, puddle iron, run a store?
Did you teach or preach? Love but leave no heirs?
And what *reward?* The hope of those who saw your worth.

A lichened footstone reads, *Joe Washington.*
Did friends' eyes light when they hailed you so?
Did Whites assume their right to abbreviate,
to obfuscate your Bible namesake?
And what of your illustrious surname—
Did you give it to yourself?
Did Washingtons buy and sell your people?

Near your headstone, someone has placed
a crockery angel—cracked, headless, hollow inside.
Glazed white.
How she causes me to wonder about my questions.

Life Lessons

The circle of grownups turns into a circus
when her grinning uncle starts to tell.
Little Girl, in the ring now, wants to hide.
I said, *D'ya wanna see where milk comes from.*
She sees it still: Uncle jerking an udder to squirt her face.
His audience laughs. Her eyes sting.

Again her mother snaps the leather belt
against Little Girl's bare, stinging legs.
She'd left her dolls in the living room,
which, for some reason, set her mother off.

When her aunt snaps at her own mother,
Little Girl stays very still.
Old One works her lips, trying to speak,
but Little Girl knows she doesn't dare,
not and stay alive in *this* house.
Old One's blind eyes drip as she shuffles away.

Little Girl watches the neighbor girl shuffle
toward the mound of raked leaves, toss an armful,
hoot and flap her arms like Little Girl's baby brother.
I like to jump in leaf piles, Little Girl thinks,
but not like her. Pitiful retard.

Little Girl sees Mrs. Sayre frown before turning her back
on a classmate who has raised her hand to answer.
Little Girl feels kind of sorry for the girl, but then again,
It's pitiful, coming to school in a dirty dress.

Big Girl now, riding the bus to her piano lesson.
She watches the houses pass by,
recalling how, when the Negroes lived here,
the row houses with their sorry porches
used to look like they couldn't stand up by themselves.
Looks a whole lot better since "urban renewal."
She likes the name.

Boss

Mom ran ragged raising us five.
Endless days of hauling laundry,
sewing clothes, cooking meals from scratch.
And rules. Iron sheets.
Floss teeth. Don't waste a moment.
When she said it was time
to clip my nails or cut my hair,
I called on Boss,
my invisible, private grownup
who lived in the back of my closet.
Boss wanted me to deliver his orders—
No, I'd say, borrowing his boldness,
my Boss says no.
Oh, if only Boss had swept Mom up
in a romp that ruined routines and *must do*s.
Instead, Mom reached for me,
set me down in a chair,
clipped.

Boxed

Dogs for boys.
Big brother with scruffy spaniels,
Uncle's hunting hounds,
the cracked photo of Dad
patting his shaggy friend.

After I asked for a kitten,
Tuxedo arrived in a bib-front shirt,
white paws as spotless
as the cotton gloves
I wore to church on Sunday.

After they brought home
another brother,
they claimed Tuxedo
sprang into the crib,
hissed and clawed.

After he disappeared,
I couldn't pry
the secret loose until
they thought
my grief had dried,

when they told me
Dad drove my boxed kitty
down the highway
and tossed him out.

I loved them all.

Retroflection

What I did was so confounding,
it grew hidden tentacles
that sucked on shame my body held
but consciousness, heart,
or wherever mind lives
could not contain.

Until recently, when a young friend
entrusted her story to me
and called what happened by its name.
After half a century, my story unwound.
I still tripped on the word for it,
so strange to own—

A man I left with after a film
at the Museum of Modern Art
and another man he brought along
a second time, without asking.
The two of them whispering
as they poured wine, laced it with something
I couldn't see, then stoked a bong.

I was wild back then, I told myself
while career, husband, kids raised right—
all lashed to my anchored pain.
When I (seldom) allowed the ugly memory,
I looked at it the same way—
I chose to go.

Losing It

After my first lover left, I lost the keys to the car
I agreed to share until he could find a job.
He had gambled away my savings on the sly.
Endings are complicated.

Years later, a necklace my husband gave me
disappeared after his horrid death,
while I was locked in *No Exit* hell
with several who sought to steal everything.
Fear slithered in again, rattling
under legal wrangling, illness. Even mail,
like the letter from a medical lab that read,
We regret a security breach . . .

Later, when COVID struck, poisoning the world,
someone slipped into my computer
to infect the brain that held my writing life.
Pneumonia nearly took me.
But here's the thing:
I found my necklace
nestled in a pouch I had so secretly stowed
I lost the memory.

Joan of Arc's Testament

My saints also spoke to me of my body.
Strong. A boy's muscled frame.
The stamina of a woman in labor.
A maid, yes,
then out of bounds of my estate.
After I walked many leagues, for months,
all my bleeding stopped.
Instead of babes,
I would bear armor.
My breasts molded to brace
a crossbow.
Limbs lissome to guide my horse.
Beyond the reach of hungry, tired,
can't-push-on-ahead.
My men calling me small
only made me smile.
What is small?
Dreams cut down by limitation.
Horizons that end with sight—
Why not seek the King?
Still, it was never just about winning,
but some theurgy in motion.
I was made to cross.
The flames, the ire of paltry men.

Here Remembering Araju, Killed at 17

Encountering Molly Vaughan's "Project 42: Gwen Amber Rose Araju, Newark, CA, 2021."

The artist and her team create garments that commemorate the lives of murdered transgender and gender-nonconforming individuals. Using Google Earth, Vaughan takes screen shots of locations where these murders have occurred. She manipulates the digital images to make abstract patterns . . . printing them on fabric . . .
—National Museum of Women in the Arts, 2024

How the artists transferred
maps marking murder onto cloth wallpaper
that transforms the room.
Transfusion of compassion.

Patterned cloth multiplies the violence,
the grief,
Araju's courage to reveal themself.
How transfigured screen shots memorialize their life.

How the artists stitched a tunic, here suspended,
shape-shifting as we who are alive stir the air.
Reminders that Gwen Amber Rose once dressed
and undressed each day a body
that transported their never-to-be-recreated self.

How the dress waits for activists
to transilluminate lives
when they wear it to march, to witness,
to transfix hate. Burn through hatred

as a magnifying glass on this wallpaper,
focusing the sun's power,

would burn it up if,
if the cloth were no longer needed
to focus our attention.

Ashes rising on a transcendental breeze would grieve.

Wisdom

my newborn
sucked and screamed

when I cried
the doctor laughed
mothers forget he said

my breasts burning
cracked
in a room with yellow wallpaper

a stolid spouse shushing me
calm down now dear

dear my five-times mother
far away
muted

by mid-century doctors' theft
of mother wisdom

she was old before she told
of terror alone in a hospital room

where at 42 she bore
my final brother
she hadn't wanted

back home
her breasts wept

postpartum depression
just now named

I write this because

Amar's Last Visit

For my mother and her caregivers

To come to an end.
When progress stops,
insurance will not pay
for me to give you PT,
he tells her.
He lays her head
back on the pillow,
slides his other arm
from behind slack shoulders.
She loves him for binding
her almost blank pages
with the bright cover
of lessons
after she could no longer
rise
even by gripping her walker handles,
shoving off,
grunting up
to shuffle beside Bela, her companion,
down the hall to chair yoga,
which she loved
for the air stirred there
with dancing legs
and arms waving
like so many hallelujahs.
When progress stops.

When, after a life of grit,
effort no longer
summons the strength
to relearn, regain, leave pain.
How to roll onto one side,
swing both legs down,
lift a head heavy with memory,
hand-walk to lift
the rest of her
to sitting.
Bela will have to hoist her
by the armpits.

Stained Glass in Köln

. . . nothing here below is profane, for everything is sacred.
—Pierre Teilhard de Chardin, *The Divine Milieu*

Rain has settled on the skylight.
As sun reappears, small pools glisten,
glass beads in a vase.
They quiver to the purring of my Rhine-moored ship.

I've just come from the cathedral, the city's jewel.
Regal, alone in a square
once crowded with buildings crumbled in World War II.
How could a single stone survive?
My eyes climbed the spires, heaven-bound tracery,
impossible lace.
Alas, ash-coated, soot-soiled.

Inside, the transept window drew me.
Countless small, random fragments,
shards that tell, not biblical stories,
but the glory of gold, red, orange, blue.
The panes insist on the present and also aver,
We went blind when our ancient glass exploded,
tearing flesh, stabbing the eyes of passersby.
We remember. We sing.

Polyphony of color has returned with me to the ship,
in the sunlit firmament of raindrops overhead.
God's palette, God's hand.

Peaceable Kingdom

The farm he grew up on stirred in my father
all the years he worked in a federal building
near the National Mall.
Nice days, he took his paper-bag lunch to a park bench,
then strode along the green expanse
until it was time to shut himself inside again.

One summer day, the Smithsonian folk festival was in full swing,
the Mall roasting like in Arkansas
where Dad learned early to sweat behind a mule and plow.

Walking more slowly because of the heat,
he heard an auctioneer's staccato babble.
Spur of the moment, Dad trotted up and raised the bid
just as others began to drop out.
Who'd want a cabin of hand-hewn logs,
no caulking, crude floor, no door?
The planks would have to be hauled and reset.
300, 350, 450, 500, the auctioneer rattled on
until maybe he saw Dad's eyes smile.
Sold to the man holding up a paper bag!

Dad was both practical and a dreamer.
When he had a spare dollar, he put it on top of Mom's
until there was a pile tall enough to buy another house to rent out.
Once the mortgage was paid,
the rental income sent another one of us through college.

By the time of the cabin era, most of us were grown
and the dreamer in Dad held more sway.
He'd bought thirty acres along a stream.
The one-room shelter offered plenty to glory in
when he and my little brother went to fish
and bed down amid the sunset-singing robins,
soughing trees, roosting turkeys' peaceable gobble.

II.
Perspective

Watershed

Encountering Andy Goldsworthy's "Watershed"
at deCordova Sculpture Park

Where is art in a hut in the woods

Come closer

Masons cut stones for walls
without mortar

Crevices between each undulating layer
might be stream beds   veins

Enter the shed   where your hands want to trace
a maze carved in the granite back wall
that braces the hillside

In the center   a dark hole
earthen tunnel that sought a spring   mineral-infused
to dye the mural face it trickles down

Consider   a shepherd's hut   hermitage   stable
invitation to imagine
headwaters of creation

Figure and Ground

Meditation in the Museum of Indian Arts and Culture,
Santa Fe, New Mexico

Riding on and on, the weary Spaniards glimpse,
through shimmering heat, fields and nearly naked men.
Beyond, a cliff gridded with ladders.

The farmers stop hoeing,
astonishment swirling among them—strangers
encased in robes and silver, weapons flashing.

An elder sends a runner to the village.
The travelers follow, dismount, and climb
to dark rooms where bare-breasted women bow

and offer cups of cool water. Encircling adobe walls,
baskets and rugs—and their creators—
remember when they were greening yucca and roaming game.

The foreigners sup from etched and painted pottery
that plays across borders—black patterns on white backgrounds
and, when read another way, white designs on black geometry—

if the beholders know the art of seeing.

Earth, Breath, Water, Fire

Meditation on a bowl-making film, Museum of Indian Arts and Culture, Santa Fe, New Mexico

An aged couple circles grates laden with earthen bowls.
The potters cover the clay with cake pans,
black and dented from use, and thatch this roof
with dried cow dung. As solemn as priests,
the elders light the pyre with kindling
while their daughter, who is learning, and the ancestors
look on, seventy times seven generations firing bowls
in which to cook, store water, save seeds.
Each bowl holds the shape of hands cupped
to receive or make an offering. The fire-tenders
sweat as flames breathe and exhale smoke
when doused with dirt. With forked sticks,
the artisans unveil each piece.
Resting in sun-warmed sand, the bowls
gleam, shiny obsidian, red and black, terracotta—
each one finished by fire's benison
and their makers' humble benediction—*a good firing.*

At Nu View Stone, Inc.

Pedro invites me into his realm—
granite wrested from middle earth.

Polished slabs stand in upright rows, like books
braced by iron bookends, for browsing.

Scanning the shelves, Pedro exclaims, *Nature! Nature!*
as though trying to sum up God's universal library.

Stories of plates shifting, layers pressing, glaciers raking.
Even now, the stone only seeming to stay still.

See this piece? A map where a green river
meanders through alabaster plains.

Conceiver of cloisonné inlaid this giant jewel with mica.
A master mosaicist created that panel of peach and gold.

And yet.

Also a graveyard, where we roam among headstones,
themselves the bodies disinterred by rapacious machines.

Imagine the butchery, landscapes disemboweled.
Or a battlefield strewn with dead—Ezekiel's boneyard.

As a boy in Brazil, Pedro's *garimpeiro* father
taught him how to prospect for gems they cut and sold.

Treasures, he calls his stone collection. Also
earth's bones that he will cut for my kitchen counters.

Torn

I

Outside, Milo's wet saw whines, slicing tile,
while inside, Lucas's crowbar
breaks the old floor loose.

All day, the wailing blade,
the thwack and crack
and sandy grit I cause

by renovating rooms. More waste to fill the dump.
In me, dust, no poems for a month,
friends neglected, nerves scrap and staccato.

This re-creation does not matter.
A new look—so what? For how long?
Seven decades in, how long before I break?

Tiles clatter as Lucas drops them into a bag.
I once saw bones piled against a chapel wall
to make room for more bodies in graves.

II

Every day, bomb blasts in Gaza, Israel,
Yemen, Ukraine. Bodies. Rubble.
Nearby, at the temporary shelter

where I work, people shuffle in or doze
on stoop and curb. Living breaks them. How to mend?
The racket here in my home is the din of luxury.

Milo and Lucas nail down underflooring, then kneel
to lay new tile. Craftsmen
from another troubled country, minding dreams.

Tile glaziers, saw makers, richly stocked stores
buzz an economy that is a foundation—
and cracked. Build, break, build.

Perspective

Fed up with fretting over taxes, an email that stings,
and the slow drip of words that pool in my mind,
I take a walk to find what is bigger.

Lining my street, svelte, young sycamores sashay
like models down a runway. Older trees—
fat, knuckled, speckle-barked—willingly

upstaged. Their own limbs seem to whistle, though.
Like piercing piccolos, warblers serenade
the village of tall townhouses

that hum with stories of neighbors' lives.
Carol's, too, and Paul's, and Susan's,
who, when they died, left themselves

here among us other elders
with careers, grandkids, travel.
Joys, struggles, sorrows—some greater than mine.

In the far field, with the marsh beyond,
looms the blunt-nosed boulder Moby Dick,
big as a barge and how deep under?

The sky. Brushed with Cirrus clouds
whispering possibility. *Rain coming,*
my next-door neighbor confirms

as I walk back up my driveway.
Millions of raindrops will shower the estuary's
long neck as it winds toward the illimitable sea.

Sharing

Cradling her broken stool, the newcomer paused
at the door to look around our workroom.
I have one like that. Our visitor nodded to a rocker nearby.

A Lincoln, I said. *After Lincoln's. At the theater.*
I meant no surprise, just a little about
what furniture holds. The way lives turn.

Sticks of brittle cane dropped onto the workbench
when our client set down her stool.

Make yourself comfortable, said my wife,
running her fingers over the burled maple.
A treasure, my beloved smiled. *Hand-planed.*

My wife and I think of what people bring us as elders
coming for renewal, our customers
as partners who care what can be saved.

Our visitor moved to the counter,
lifted a jar of our honey to the light,
then the faded picture of us beside our hives.

What kind of flowers? she wanted to know.
Then, *I might try honey for my poor lungs.*

I felt the favor of her sharing.
What bees do in their short lives,
letting us partake of their sweet harvest.

Arachnids

One rappels from the eaves.
Her self-made rope sways
to and fro in August breeze.
Trapeze.
Just above, almost in reach,
caught by skin in a spin, a mite.
One bite.

One explores the storm door,
seeking—what?
Or maybe not.
Into a crevasse. Gone.
Now back again,
arms waving Durga-like.

A third scales the cedar siding,
straight, impossible up
El Capitan,
Grand Canyon wall,
Mount Rushmore,
over the chin, the nose, the brow.
Wow.

Understudy

Spider silk makes a slow-spinning mobile
of a pine needle that dangles
from the deck railing.
Cranesbill geraniums nuzzle
the lower branches of a tall spiraea
boasting profusions of fuchsia.
Rabbit, too young to fear the open air, rests,
wearing a Drishti gaze.
Invisible squirrels *chuck, chuck, chuck,*
complaining, perhaps, that my presence
disrupts a romp on their lawn.

I'm already absorbed in all that's going on
when coyote lopes out of the woods—
which of us more startled?
A mottled youth, she veers back under trees
and weaves a ghostly path through dappled shade.
Has she passed too quickly to care to catch
yonder napping chipmunk curled beneath a leaf?
Yellow moth rises from a cloud of buttery lobelia,
zigzags up, then down to disappear,
disguised as blossom. Ants meander on stage.
Red-tailed hawk swoops in, a *deus ex machina.*
I sit still, trying to learn my lines.

Saw

When does the old oak die?
Was it when the dismemberment began
with a buzzing blade
severing limbs?

Or does the tree still suffer
as the man clamps
an iron claw around the trunk?

All sentient beings, says a prayer.
Why has my neighbor ordered this?
To straighten his riding mower's path?
Make way for a backyard pool?
Protect his house from branches
wrenched loose by wind?

Slices of trunk,
suspended from a crane,
spin slowly down.
Would that the crane
were a Sandhill Crane
carrying omens.

The skinny pines behind
where the oak once spread
now look far apart.
What they know.

The policeman guarding the road
waves us on,
the line of cars a cortege.

All the Green

Tender beginnings. Unmade bed. Small wilderness.
I watched the bare ground around my new house
hint of stalk, leaf, and blade.

Come June, a vine began befriending what
by then I recognized as lilies, dianthus, phlox,
invasions of Black-eyed Susan

and much that I could not name
except to call them *weeds,* as one says *grief,*
knowing sorrows are not the same.

After the ordeals that moved me to this place—
the withering, dying, falling away—
I let all the green come in.

Later, even the jab of trowel in soil
would be the dot of a question mark:
What to let be, move, remove?

The bloom and billow of *what if*s,
musings and doubts that gather under question marks'
curved stems. This freedom, in this new place, to ask,

what questions am I?
I put away my trowel, let summer pass
amid known flowers, weeds, and wonder.

How a spreading, round-leaved thing spilled over
the garden's edge. Something silver, leaves furry as rabbit ears.
How a vine with scalloped leaves wove a lace coverlet.

And the weeds' desire. The orneriness
to go everywhere, as love does,
by runner and root, blown and falling seed.

What's in a Name

Greenhouse effect suggested
an arboretum's musky fecundity
instead of nature ruined and everybody dead.
A future I squinted to see
from Al Gore's movie or casual observation,
like out-of-season weather once in a while.
Easy to toss such miscellany into a junk drawer
with paper clips and rotting rubber bands.

Then came *global warming,* a moniker
some of us laughed at during ice storms.
Or argued with or coolly pinned to glacier cracks
and random heaves of melting permafrost—
all overshadowed by internal weather,
like the lead-cold grief that moved in
when my beloved died.

Before long came *climate change*
in deference to doomsday fires, drowning torrents,
plagues of hurricanes.
Climate change—too neutral-sounding?
Like changing a baby's diaper
or replacing oil in my gas-fed car.

Lately I hear *global weirdness,*
passed off as sarcastic shorthand
that draws attention to the speaker's wit
and downplays the immensity of doom.

Remember Bergman's film *The Seventh Seal?*
The scrape of a woodman's saw, mostly off camera,
where the grim reaper, that ageless cutup,
will topple the tree where the frightened man
the camera lingers on
has climbed to escape from danger.

Quiet

The first wave of frothy clouds breaks
on blue, which soon disappears,
flood tide.
Sun now a blur,
fading altogether within the hour.
Nuthatches, chickadees,
and bossy jays suspend their search.
Turkeys in the far field stop
their pecking meander.
This morning's squirrels, nowhere.
What we sense in the dampening air.
We huddle in the crook of a pine limb,
make a bed of fallen leaves,
burrow.
Safe, for now, in our lodgings,
we wait.
In the time of fires,
downpours, blasting wind,
a flutter at the blurry edge of fear.
Even what is foretold,
unknowable.

Reckoning

All day, wind and sheets of rain.
I hope the tree roots hold
and saturated soil brings a worm harvest
for robins gliding in to rustle grass
now greening.

How quickly my desire slides into spring.

I wonder how worms know time,
know when it is time. Robins, too.
What sense compels their flying north or south?
What is *now* except this branch to grip in storm-swept trees?

I envy them their *now.* I brood on ruination.

Will robins know when fewer broods survive?
How do whales in the nearby sea sense a dwindling tribe?
Do worms, robins, whales remember forebears, teeming?
The great leviathans *must* grieve
lost calves and cousins beached.

Conscious, and, yes, with knowledge—
robins in a dell that holds the shape of home—
synthesis of feel, scent, and sight
for this ground, leaf-bedded, spongy.

What systems let the birches know their neighbors' needs,
even, perhaps, my need of them?
What store of sonar maps do right whales carry,
though migraine-dizzy from roaring ships?

When patterns fracture, what then?
Grief I cannot reckon settles in.
Yet hope keeps showing up, greening.

The Man Interviewed on the Radio after the Christmas Blizzard in Buffalo

Wind gusting really sudden and the sky let loose.
No more customers, like a spigot turned off.
I read the paper, enjoying the pause
even though I'm used to brisk business right up to Christmas.
I cut hair, you see, men's mostly.
Sometimes boys coming in with their dads,
young ones—their fathers telling me, *Cut it short,*
and the kids won't complain.
I clip the top, shave up the neck.
Careful over those little ears.
Anyway, snow piling up fast, not even a car creeping by.
I turn on the radio.
The man is saying about people losing power
and I can hear the wind blowing something fierce,
power lines sagging like the black snake I once saw
hanging between my bird feeder and the fence.
People calling the station for help,
saying the rescue can't drive their trucks
into their part of town.
Then the windows across the street blink and go black.
Gray day fading into night and my shop still lit.

I'm sure not going anywhere,
so I clear the doorway in case of fire.
Can't win against the snow heaped on the steps—
I can hardly see the end of my shovel,
ice hitting my face like darts.
Then somebody appears from nowhere, ghostly,
weaving back and forth in the wind and all hunched over.
I call out in case they can't see me.
A woman with her cat wrapped up like in a cocoon.
Fixed hot cocoa so she could hug the mug to thaw her hands.
Decided to call in to the radio, said I still have power
and for anybody else to come over if they can.
Before long, more ghosts sliding our way,
me and the woman hardly seeing them until they stumble up
a knee-deep hill of snow where my steps were.
Pretty soon we run out of cocoa,
but glory be, in come people carrying cans—
beans, tuna, cranberry sauce,
and left-overs from warming refrigerators.
We give the tuna to the cat,
then eat a mixed-up supper with plastic spoons.
After, we call the station again, and more people blow in
lugging garbage bags with blankets, cookies—
a camping stove, of all things.

I ask, does anybody need a haircut?
Everybody laughs, but some do,
which I give the best I can, even the ladies.
I'm a barber, you see, not a hairdresser,
but everybody I gave a cut to was real kind.

Hildegard in Her Workshop

Hildegard, Prioress of Rupertsberg, known as
Hildegard of Bingen, 1098–1179

I don't remember much before I was sent away.
Helping my mother tend her flowers,
wondering, at Mass, about the voices behind the screen,
humming strands I could remember.
How Love visited in visions I did not yet understand.

When we left home,
they didn't say where they were taking me
until we could see the gate.
So many women!
Some girls, not many—Jutta, of course,
who I knew right away shared a soul with mine.
"Sister" was not just a title—how I loved all of them.

I felt safe.
Certainly, there were rules upon rules,
but on the outside, so many more for girls.
Deportment, chores, tedious womanly arts,
and only one path to tread—
toward marriage and bearing and bearing.
And if I lived through the birthing,
raising how many?
Every girl ending up
ruled over, worn out, if not dead.

Here I create tinctures and poultices
for people who come for our help.
I grow every kind of herb,
write down what heals.
Chants and poems glide through me,
like swallows winging into the cloister garden
to sing, as I teach my sisters to do.
I write books of melody and my mysterious intimations.
Here, I compose myself.

In Her Choir

for E. Gray

She stops playing to help us place an accidental
that sagged. After a once-through a cappella, a nod.
Now let's turn this into music, she says.
Lifting her arms, she aims us toward arc of phrase,
paradox of soft and strong, passion kindling in pianissimo.

Midway through the next piece, she plays a wrong note.
My brain is mush; she laughs at herself.
We notice her scrolling arpeggios in the right hand,
stacking thick chords in the left—
all while making a mental list of *our* several mistakes.

And we are singing in her eleventh workday hour
of meetings, practice at the organ,
searches for music that will weave liturgy
into God-animated dialogue.

I bungle an eighth-note rest. *Mea culpa,* I admit.
You'll get it, she smiles, *sans* sarcasm or reproach.
Love, her figured bass above which float
forbearance, forgiveness, gratitude.

At the organ on Sunday, as she layers a fugue,
one imagines two hands dancing with miracle feet—
or maybe two of her
tuning beauty in measured ephemera.

She carries her gifts in the direction of perfection,
knowing that practice does not make perfect,
only nearer, nearer, as melodies rise
and silence sounds. Because time bears music
that wants to continue being born.

Lost in Translation

Faithful mother tongue,
perhaps after all it's I who must try to save you.
—Czeslaw Milosz, "My Faithful Mother Tongue"

Sometimes his sons make melody with him, but often
his solo voice must suffice until
next week, when his parents call him.
Or his brother, also an *émigré,* who phones when he can
because the Thai sun is sinking as New York's lifts.
He likes to hear his family say—anything—
les huîtres for dinner, fresh from the coast,
A plan for travel to *la fête de la musique à Lyon.*
He writes film scripts in flawless Brooklyn argot,
can mimic a Texan, but when, in English, he renders
the fish mongers calling in *La Place des Lices,*
the murmurs of passersby along the canal—
to his own ears, he is a soundtrack badly dubbed.
In French, *om* the vowels, incarnate consonants,
home the long Breton summer twilight its song.

Return Flight

Everywhere laptops, tablets,
screens we were assigned to.
The Cyclopses my neighbors stare at—
adventure, horror, cartoons, news.
Small, flat people mime and speak
what only the earmuff wearer hears.

I cannot see the sky.
My eyes flit to
a drab ceiling,
a narrow aisle,
the gray shoulder of the seat
in front where a fly rests,
rubbing her palms together.
How did she slip by
the bomb-checking wands
and watched queue
at the mouth of the skyway?
Which is actually a tunnel
into this sealed ship
unmoored from
earth and time.
Am I yet in France?
Over endless waves?

Screens go blind *in medias res*
when the pilot, in hard English,
warns of a bumpy ride.
In my mind's ear, music
I'm used to, French.

How a sentence climbs, crests,
then feather-falls.
How each query lifts up
to the question mark’s
curved dome,
where it waits.

To Fly

To fly, as I am now, aboard
a jet, and all the while
be out of time in infinitives
that float, suspended,
nowhere past or yet.

To streak, Boston to Boise,
travel back in time,
arrive two hours behind.
To envision what lies ahead—
the waiting arms of a beloved friend.

While sitting still, to play
in the circus of language,
turning nouns into verbs—
to tightrope,
to highwire.

Or costume verbs as nouns
that slide, chameleon-like,
through sentences where
to be
is to be camouflaged.

To be at once rooted
in the bedrock of syntax
and unbound.

To take hold
of an unreeling sentence string—
to choose to tether
to past, present, progressive,
or the future now
ballooning.

III.
Ever

Picking Up

Balancing on the piano keys, an iridescent marble
set down when Emile played the Star Wars theme.
A Lego windshield winks at me from the floor.

What my grandsons blew by when they swept up
their toys before tornadoing out the door.

Pausing beside their car, Marcel and Emile
wrapped themselves around me.
A sandwich hug, meaning, made for each other, a BLT.

When they come for vacation, I make it mine, too. This time,
spotting camouflaged clues on a hunt in the ship museum.

In the hall fitted with mast and sails, I played the wind,
jerking the yardarm to and fro while the boys perched on a rope,
giggling, small arms reaching down to haul the heavy canvas sail.

Leaving rules in ruins, we gobbled mousse for lunch,
shared an ice cream sundae at three.

Back to my orderly house, now still and silent as I pick up
a marble warmed by the palm of the one who cradled it,
a windshield waiting to join the Lego helicopter it needs.

Rust

I emptied the baggie on the counter at the jeweler's,
as bright and metallic as a morgue.
I had forgotten the watch was in pieces.
Did you claw it off the day your mind
cleft in a sepsis climax?
The lug can be soldered, the jeweler said,
but the crown is loose, escapement off, insides rusty.
I intended the keepsake for our nephew Jon,
meant to celebrate how both of you
could bring to life any mechanical thing.
But after Jon died, before the giving,
I could think of no one else.

I resorted to a shop with a crude sign,
We buy gold and silver.
A dented desk, chair hemorrhaging stuffing,
dusty trinkets scattered about.
Nothing like your workshop lined with tools
for perfecting your creations.

The grizzly proprietor smothered
the watch face with tobacco-stained fingers,
and pinched a monocle into his eye—
18 karat. I'll give you 60 bucks.
Bucks. Bluebeard smacked his lips.
I carried the pieces home.
The band holds the curve of your wrist.

In Strasbourg Cathedral

You stir as I cross the threshold
from searing sun into somber nave.
Here you are,
close enough to hear me whisper,
You would like this.

I can translate for you—
how I came by way of Rue Déserte—
yes, deserted, only it wasn't.
And Rue des Serruriers,
where long-ago craftsmen
fashioned keys and locks
for sundry chests and doors.

Mesdames et Messieurs,
A solemn voice intones,
Shshsh.

Let us sit;

the Mass begins.
You will recognize the outlines—
Call to Worship, Lessons, Sanctus, Supper.

We will gaze at the pleasing lines
of gently sloping arches,
conceived on the cusp of two eras in design.
The church's spine.

I remember yours.

I wonder, shall I light a votive?
But it would be commemoration only,
whereas, for a little while just now,
I held your flame.

Ghosted

I wake up drenched in dread
There you sit at your desk in the cellar
designing circuits that look like desolate streets
You show no sign you see the pain you caused me
by never daring to unsnarl the tangled wires
in dear ones you might have helped

They stand near you   driving verbal rivets
as usual   oblivious to you and me
while their motor-mouths grind on
When their batteries run down
you look at me blankly and say *No   no*

You don't remember ignoring me
when I couldn't shake off pneumonia
all summer before you died
nor how   when I nursed you to the end
you fought me to exhaustion
while you took care that your work would live
and left all else untended

Now you chide me for throwing out
your box of rusted screws
before I sold the house
and moved away to free myself

You want to go on
as if you hadn't created this mess
as if you hadn't died
Please   I say to the dark
Let me be

Simpatico

On a cruise with mostly couples
a stranger I sat next to suggested
an appetizer to her husband.
He frowned at her, jerked his indignant chin,
and barked a different order.

For most of the trip, I hung out with two couples,
all engineers and best friends.
At meals, we kidded with our affable waiter
and joked about who ate more chocolate.
We took turns deciding what to explore on shore—

the way you and I used to. We were *simpatico,* mostly,
except when you slipped into your father's skin.
Your dad and mom were *hand in glove,* you bragged.
His hand, her pliant glove, I thought, but never said.

If you were still alive, would you even remember
that night, out with the Governor and his wife?
You know how women are, you said, winking at the Gov.
Later, in the car, you had no idea and mumbled, *Sorry,*
as you flicked a breadcrumb from your tie.

At the end of my cruise, in a lecture
on the ship's navigation, I showed my curiosity.
A husband turned to the captain, grinned,
and gave himself permission to say,
Well now, isn't she quite the little engineer.

Still lurking, what lies coiled among us.

Forgiveness

I

You have been the last and hardest to deal with,
slouching around corners
so that I barely glimpse your back.
Sometimes only visible seasonally and on clear nights,
and like the Pleiades, by looking to the side.

I've known your angry twin for years.
She bounded in when I was betrayed, and stayed,
lithe, scruffy, a restless thing
whose snarl sounds like courage.
I like to watch her charge and lunge.

Are you two closer than I used to think?
You, the inscrutable one—sphinx, blinking star,
silent stalker, shoulder-shrugging doppelgänger,
crouching to lick my foot or bare your teeth
before you slink away again for weeks.

Lately you've been loitering,
mewling under the porch.
What if I set out milk each day—or meat?
I admit I'm scared to start.
What if you slip in the door and stay?

Promise me that when you curl on the couch,
wind yourself around my ankles,
put on weight, show claws,
you'll let your sister keep tearing around,
sharing my heart with pain.

II

Or forgiveness

may be not created in the way I thought,
that is, arising in spontaneous generation
from my release of those who wronged me

maybe not coming in this life, even

may be accepting that karmic resonance,
while what I do causes some vibration,
goes on beyond my will or action, impartial, even

maybe not coming in this life, even

may be perpetual and comingled
with crimes, not undone, my wise anger,
and all cosmic stir, indivisible,

beyond my control in how they flow,
where they go.

Ever

You again, uninvited,
arm raised to knock
when I happen to see you at the door.
The same raised brow,
mouth a surprised O, as on your last day,
when you saw the end.
You will die again on Thursday, All Saints' Eve.

I still ponder your reply—
instead of *I love you, too,*
a pause. And then, *I expect you'll manage.*
Is grief ever just sorrow?

I've remodeled the final two rooms.
Yes, you would have managed this project.
The man I hired,
I might have fallen for if he were not already
married to a woman he admires,
as you admired me.
Does sorrow ever resolve?

I've just returned from France
where I spent the Euros
you kept for the next trip we never took.
Near the end of my stay,
I happened upon the oldest garden.

Suddenly, in front of me—the inn
where you and I stayed.
The wrought iron balcony,
French doors open, curtains dancing.

Remember the dour proprietor
who seemed incapable of smiling?
Until I called her russet, pointy-nosed dog
Maître Renard and recited
the opening of La Fontaine's fable.
For a moment, our three grinning faces rhymed.

Designs for Life

When my mother roused her treadle to sew, I flew
to my dress-ups to don the dress she was married in—
eyelet, the color of heliopsis. She greeted me
the southern way, as *Missus,* and spooled out questions
that I used to stitch my stories cut from clouds
she billowed with fulsome *aah*s and *is that so*s—
the same as when other housewives came to chat.
From ingenuity and the fabric of circumstance,
we improvised our days. Later, as a grownup,
I met a handsome stranger. We pieced together
scraps of conversation that we quilted into love.
Now he is gone and I grow old, asking
what new fancies will arise? What dress
will daybreak wear to play with day?

Gift

A friend's gait is wobbly; another has worn-out knees.
Mine, creaky as I trot beside my grandson Marcel.
Why are your teeth black, he wants to know.
Tea stains I can barely see.
Still, I know myself better now—
how to let go of small slights,
how to catch the thief inside
who tries to snatch my self-esteem.
How to touch serenity by naming daily blessings
as I tap each bead on the large bangle
Marcel created as a toddler,
generously threading bright plastic on a pipe cleaner.
He evidently thought the stiff hoop would fit
my grownup wrist—thin, eroding tracery.
Or maybe he saw, but imagined me anyway,
sturdy and always.
When I was raising his mother,
all the unlovely imperfect, I threw away—
macaroni necklaces, crooked origami,
a coat-hanger mobile bearded with yarn.
Now, love's ambitious project, I save.

About the Author

Winner of Orison Books' 2023 Best Spiritual Literature poem prize and a *Naugatuck River Review* 2024 Best Narrative Poem finalist, Merryn Rutledge is widely published. Her previous collection is *Sweet Juice and Ruby-Bitter Seed* (Kelsay Books, 2023). Merryn teaches poetry craft, reviews new poetry books, and volunteers for social justice.

After teaching literature and creative writing for many years at Phillips Exeter Academy, she earned a doctorate in leadership and ran a US-based leadership development consulting firm. During this period, Merryn's writing on her field work in leadership was published in peer-reviewed journals, as book chapters, and as books.

Website:
merrynpoetry.org

www.ingramcontent.com/pod-product-compliance
Lightning Source LLC
LaVergne TN
LVHW090616110826
845146LV00001B/414